NATURE
IN
FOCUS

LIFE IN A
CORAL REEF

By Jen Green

Gareth Stevens
Publishing

Please visit our Web site www.garethstevens.com. For a free color catalog of all our high-quality books, call toll free 1-800-542-2595 or fax 1-877-542-2596.

Library of Congress Cataloging-in-Publication Data

Green, Jen.
    Life in a coral reef / Jen Green.
      p. cm. -- (Nature in focus)
    Includes index.
    ISBN 978-1-4339-3423-0 (library binding) -- ISBN 978-1-4339-3424-7 (pbk.)
    ISBN 978-1-4339-3425-4 (6-pack)
    1. Coral reefs and islands--Juvenile literature. 2. Coral reef ecology--Juvenile literature.
    I. Title.
    GB461.G74 2010
    578.77'89--dc22
                            2009038716

Published in 2010 by
Gareth Stevens Publishing
111 East 14th Street, Suite 349
New York, NY 10003

© 2010 The Brown Reference Group Ltd.

For Gareth Stevens Publishing:
Art Direction: Haley Harasymiw
Editorial Direction: Kerri O'Donnell

For The Brown Reference Group Ltd:
Editorial Director: Lindsey Lowe
Managing Editor: Tim Harris
Editor: Jolyon Goddard
Children's Publisher: Anne O'Daly
Design Manager: David Poole
Designer: Lorna Phillips
Picture Manager: Sophie Mortimer
Picture Researcher: Clare Newman
Production Director: Alastair Gourlay

Picture Credits:
Front Cover: Getty Images; Photographers Choice; istockphoto:(background)
BRG: Lorna Philips: 31; istockphoto: 20; Johan Anderson: 20; C. Dascher: 24; Jupiter Images: Photos.com: 9; Stockxpert: 28; Shutterstock: Rich Carey: 3, 10, 19, 29; CB Pix: 23; Mark Doherty: 24; Marcus Elfer: 21; Tyler Fox: 8; Peter Leahy: 12; Tatyana Morozava: 30; Hisom Silviu: 16; Segey Skleznev: 18; Dwight Smith: 17; Niikita Tiunov: 13; Kerry L. Werry: 14
All Artworks Brown Reference Group

Manufactured in the United States of America
1 2 3 4 5 6 7 8 9 12 11 10

CPSIA compliance information: Batch #BRW0102GS: For further information contact Gareth Stevens, New York, New York at 1-800-542-2595.

Contents

Reefs Around the World   **4**

Life on a Reef   **6**

The Coral Kingdom   **8**

Bright Colors, Amazing Shapes   **16**

Predators and Prey   **24**

Getting to Know Reefs   **30**

Glossary   **32**

Index   **32**

Reefs Around the World

The undersea gardens of coral reefs support thousands of colorful sea animals. Some reefs are giant rocky structures that rise through the water like skyscrapers. The largest reefs are so big they can be seen from space—yet they are built by tiny animals. This book will introduce you to the amazing animals that live on reefs around the world.

Most of the world's coral reefs are located near the equator.

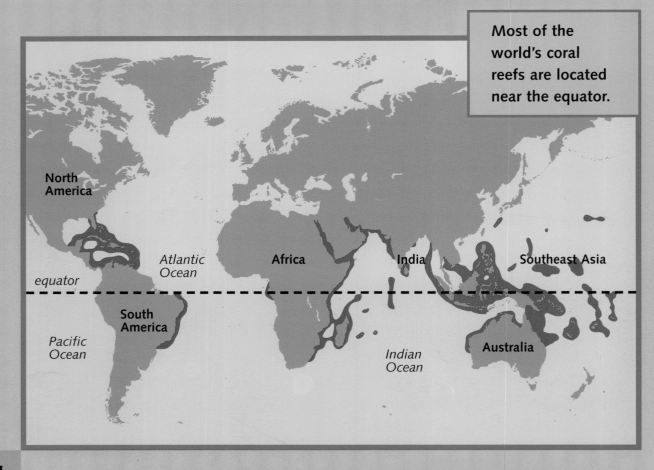

North America

Atlantic Ocean

Africa

India

Southeast Asia

equator

South America

Pacific Ocean

Indian Ocean

Australia

Sponges often grow on coral reefs. Like corals, sponges are animals, and some sponges look similar to the corals themselves.

Some parts of the world have many coral reefs. There are more than 50 reefs near southern Florida.

Life on a Reef

barracuda

remora

shark

shark

moray eel

Coral reefs are full of life. Nearly one-quarter of all ocean **species** live on or around coral reefs. Reef-building corals can live only in sunlit shallow waters that stay warm all year. Fringe reefs form off coasts and islands; barrier reefs also occur along coasts but lie farther out to sea. Atolls are circular reefs around sunken islands.

Coral reefs can be divided into zones. In each zone, the temperature and the amount of sunlight that reaches through the water varies. Each zone has a different set of animals that lives there.

Tiny animals called coral **polyps** build reefs. Sponges and sea anemones attach themselves to the rocky surface. Thousands of small animals live on the reef.

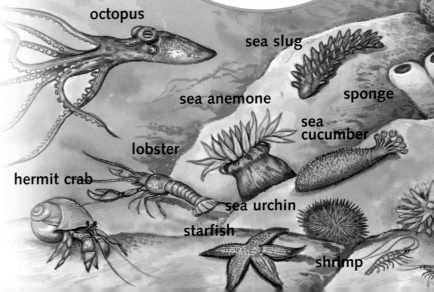

octopus

sea slug

sea anemone

sponge

sea cucumber

lobster

hermit crab

sea urchin

starfish

shrimp

6

loggerhead turtle

triggerfish

long-nosed butterfly fish

butterfly fish

The reef is an excellent hunting ground for large predators, such as sharks and barracuda. Prey fish have many ways to avoid being eaten.

angelfish

copepod (animal plankton)

surgeonfish

squirrelfish

brain coral

staghorn coral

Bright, beautiful fish, such as angelfish and surgeonfish, weave their way among waving sea fans and sponges. Their bold stripes and markings blend in with the shadows of the reef.

parrot fish

The Coral Kingdom

Coral reefs are made of the skeletons of billions of tiny coral polyps. Some large reefs have taken millions of years to form. A polyp is a small animal with a soft, tube-shaped body. At the top of its body is a ring of stinging tentacles that it uses to capture food. In reef-building corals, the bottom of the polyp is not soft but hard and stony.

Coral reefs are built by tiny animals called coral polyps. They survive only in clear, warm, shallow waters.

Coral reefs are fragile. Boats and ships can damage hundreds of years of coral growth if they run aground on a reef.

This large, branching elkhorn coral grows toward the sunlight at the surface of the water.

Reef Builders

Reef-building coral polyps take in a chemical called calcium bicarbonate from the surrounding water. Each polyp then makes a substance called calcium carbonate to make a white, cup-shaped shell under the thin layer of flesh on the underside of its body. This hard, and sometimes brittle, chalky shell anchors the polyp to the reef. When the polyp dies, its skeleton remains. Over years, the reef slowly grows as the polyp skeletons build up, layer upon layer.

As a reef builds up, the layers of polyp skeletons are gradually crushed. Eventually, they turn into a hard rock called limestone.

Stony and Soft Corals

There are many different kinds of corals. Some types of hard corals are shaped like saucers or grooved pillars. Brain corals look like a human brain. Only some hard, or stony, corals build coral reefs.

Soft corals and their relatives sea fans have delicate orange, yellow, or purple leaflike fronds that sway gently in the ocean currents. Tiny grains of calcium carbonate, called spicules, strengthen the bodies of these corals. Soft corals and sea fans are sometimes shaped like deer antlers or fans.

Of the several thousand species of corals, fewer than 1,000 of them are reef-building stony corals.

Many types of animals live on coral reefs. One reef in Key Largo, Florida, has more than 550 different animal species.

Coral Reef Zones

Reefs can be divided into different zones. The reef crest is the highest point. Behind it, between the reef and the shore, lies a **lagoon** of warm, shallow, sunlit water. On the other side, the reef slopes down to a depth of 150 feet (45 m). The various zones support different types of life. Flatfish, crabs, and sea urchins live on the sandy seabed behind the crest. Barnacles cling to the top of the reef. Sea anemones, sponges, fish, and clams crowd the seaward reef slopes.

The world's longest coral reef is the Great Barrier Reef. It runs 1,240 miles (2,000 km) along the northeastern coast of Australia.

THE REEF AT NIGHT

Divers who swim in the sunlit waters of the coral reef by day get to see only some of its wildlife. Many reef animals are nocturnal, or active at night. During the day, sea cucumbers, sea slugs, starfish, and snails lie low in the reef's many cracks and crannies. When night falls, they come out to look for food. Some coral polyps are also nocturnal. In the daytime, these polyps are tightly closed, but at night they open up and spread their tentacles to snare microscopic animals called zooplankton.

Sea Anemones and Mollusks

Reef animals include some that stay in one place and those that move very little. Sea anemones grip the reef with a sticky structure on their base called a pedal disk. Mollusks such as giant clams, oysters, scallops, and mussels also make their home on coral reefs. They attach themselves using a muscular "foot." Most clams and mussels are **filter feeders** and eat by sifting the water for tiny animals known as zooplankton.

In some places, the Great Barrier Reef crest towers 500 feet (150 m) above the seabed—that's as tall as a 40-story building.

Slow Movers

Starfish, crabs, and sea snails crawl over the reef in search of food. Some sea urchins, sea slugs, and marine snails such as conches are vegetarians. They nibble on seaweed. Other reef animals are meat-eating predators. A few others feed on the coral itself.

> Reef-building corals cannot live in deep seas because the algae inside them can survive only in shallow, sunlit waters.

CORAL MUNCHERS

Parrot fish eat coral by breaking off pieces of living coral with their beaklike mouths. Then they grind up the hard, chalky parts of the polyps to get a type of **algae** called zooxanthellae from inside. Some starfish also feed on living corals. They crawl over the reef, releasing chemicals that dissolve the polyps' bodies. The dissolved bodies make a polyp soup that the starfish eat. In the Pacific and Indian oceans, giant crown-of-thorns starfish prey on living coral. These spiny animals swarm over the coral, eating and leaving behind large, bare patches.

Bright Colors, Amazing Shapes

Reef animals come in all the colors of the rainbow. For some animals, their bright patterns act as a warning to predators. The fish of the reef have many different shapes. Most fish have tapering, streamlined bodies, so they move easily through the water. Others, such as sea horses and pipefish, have unusual shapes.

Sea horses use their tail as an anchor when they feed. They wrap it firmly around corals or underwater grasses.

Living coral reefs cover about 360,000 square miles (930,000 sq km) of the world's oceans—that's an area the size of Texas and Colorado combined.

Colorful fish dart around the corals like beautiful birds flying among rain forest trees.

In this picture of a butterfly fish, you can see its slender snout and the bold stripes on its head, tail, and top fin.

The coral reefs in the Florida Keys are the third largest barrier reef system in the world.

Colors and Markings

Many animals on coral reefs have colored patterns or bold markings on their bodies. These markings can warn predators not to eat them because they taste bad or are even poisonous. Other body markings help animals **camouflage** themselves by blending in with their surroundings so they cannot be seen easily. Some fish have dark spots called eyespots, which look like eyes, near their tail. These markings can fool enemies into attacking the wrong end of the fish, allowing it to escape.

Bold Stripes

Many fish have bold stripes running vertically or horizontally along their bodies. These markings break up their bodies' outlines, helping them hide among corals and seaweeds. In the open water, these same markings make the fish stand out clearly. That is very useful during the breeding season, when the fish try to attract others of the same species. They swim out in the open water to attract their mates and frighten away rival fish.

About 800 shipwrecks lie on the reefs in the Florida Keys. Some of the wrecks date back as far as the 1500s.

Sergeant majors are named for their markings, which look like the stripes on the badge of a sergeant major in the army.

Male and Female

The males and females of some fish that make their home on reefs are different colors. For example, in one type of parrot fish, the male fish are green, while females are black, white, and red. They look so different from each other that scientists once thought the fish belonged to separate species. The colors make it easy for the parrot fish to find mates. Some parrot fish can even change from being females into males if there are no suitable males to mate with during the breeding season!

Coral colonies grow very slowly. They lay down only about $\frac{1}{2}$ inch (1 cm) of growth each year.

Some adult angelfish, such as this French angelfish, are a different shape and color when they are young.

Changing Color

Bottom-dwelling fish such as flounder have mottled colors that blend in with the ocean floor. They can slowly change the color of their skin as they move from rock to sand, keeping them camouflaged from predators and also their prey—such as shrimp. Cuttlefish can change color quickly, turning from brown to beige, orange, or green in an instant. Their bodies ripple with color as they creep along the bottom in search of food.

Some coral reefs are 40 to 50 million years old. These ancient reefs are made up of coral that is $\frac{3}{4}$ mile (1.2 km) thick.

CLEANING SERVICE

On some coral reefs, small fish called cleaner wrasse provide an amazing service for larger fish. They nibble **parasites** that infest the body of their "client." The larger fish recognize the cleaners and allow them to approach and feed unharmed and even swim inside their mouths to search for parasites. Both partners benefit from this relationship—the wrasse get a free meal, and the client fish is rid of pesky parasites. Sometimes the larger fish line up patiently at a wrasse's cleaning station until the smaller fish is ready to clean!

Many cleaner wrasse have bright stripes along or down their bodies. These stripes help distinguish them from other fish. Other fish called false cleaners have similar patterns. They fool the client fish into letting them approach, then they bite the big fish and swim away!

Reef Partners

Anemone fish, or clown fish, are brightly colored fish that live among the stinging tentacles of sea anemones. The tentacles are venomous and can paralyze other fish, but the clown fish is covered with slimy mucus, which probably protects it from the stings. Clown fish live and rear their young among the waving tentacles, safe from predators. The sea anemone benefits, too. The fish hoover up scraps of food that the sea anemone cannot digest, keeping its tentacles clean and healthy. In addition, the sea anemone gets nutrients from the fish's wastes.

Scientists think that the Florida Keys reefs formed about 125,000 years ago, during a time known as the Pleistocene Age.

Remoras attach themselves to sharks by a sucker on their head. They then get free rides and scraps of food.

Predators and Prey

Some animals on the coral reef are herbivores, or plant eaters, that eat algae and sea grasses. Many are carnivores, or meat eaters. Some feed on **carrion** and do not catch live prey. They are known as scavengers. Usually, the smallest animals of the reef are eaten by medium-size hunters, which fall prey to larger predators.

Whale sharks are not fierce predators despite their huge size. They filter feed on plankton, tiny fish, and shrimp.

Barracuda have excellent eyesight and are fierce hunters on Florida's coral reefs.

As these fish turn through the water, light reflects off their scales. That confuses predators and makes them difficult to catch.

CORAL REEF FOOD CHAIN

This diagram, right, shows an example of a food chain in and around a coral reef. Tiny, plantlike plankton are the base of this chain. Tiny copepods (part of the animal plankton) feed on the plantlike plankton; shrimp eat the copepods; angelfish eat the shrimp; and larger fish, such as barracuda, eat the smaller fish. At the top of the food chain are the most fearsome hunters—big sharks.

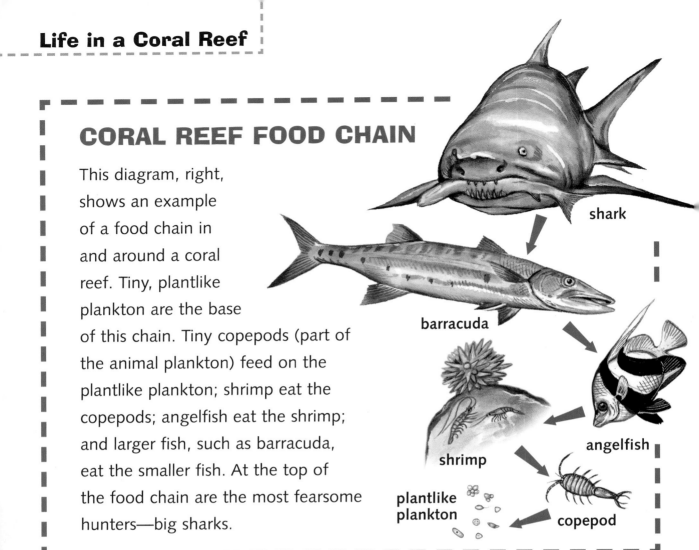

shark

barracuda

shrimp

plantlike plankton

angelfish

copepod

Top Hunters

At the top of each reef food chain are large predators such as sharks. Hunters of the open ocean, such as tuna and dolphins, also patrol the deep waters off the reef. Barracuda are common on reefs. These giants grow up to 12 feet (3.5 m) long and have razor-sharp teeth. Sometimes they follow human divers, but they rarely attack.

Barracuda are sometimes called the "tigers of the sea" because they are ferocious predators.

Toothy Sharks

Sharks are predators that swim in all oceans. Mako and tiger sharks have sometimes attacked people, but most sharks are harmless to humans. Hammerhead sharks are among the strangest-looking fish in the oceans. Their eyes and nostrils are mounted on large, fleshy projections that form a giant "T." Scientists believe this helps them track their prey. A shark's main weapon is its sharp teeth, used for gripping slippery fish and slicing through flesh.

Like cuttlefish and flounders, some groupers can change their color to blend in with their background.

Tiger groupers feed on smaller fish. In turn, groupers fall prey to sharks and barracuda.

REEFS IN DANGER

Coral reefs face huge threats to their survival. Some of these threats are natural, but many are caused by humans. Stocks of reef fish have dwindled because of overfishing, which upsets the natural balance of the food chains. Sewage from cities and chemicals from farms and factories **pollute** the reef waters. Sometimes, storms and rough seas smash the coral. Snorkelers and divers may also damage reefs.

Many scientists believe that global warming—the increase in the temperature of Earth's atmosphere—is destroying huge areas of coral reefs. Warmer water causes ocean algae to multiply. The algae produce chemicals that harm the coral. It then loses its own live-in algae and becomes white, or "bleached." Global warming has also made the oceans more acidic, and that reduces the growth of reefs.

When threatened, sea slugs will squirt ink into the water to confuse their attacker. That gives the sea slug time to escape.

In recent years, more than 50 percent of the Florida Keys coral has died.

Self-Protection

Animals of the coral reef have many ways of avoiding danger and protecting themselves. Fish such as herring and grunts swim in large groups called schools. These groups provide safety in numbers. As the whole school twists and turns as a glittering mass, a predator finds it difficult to single out individual fish to attack. Surgeonfish are armed with sharp spines that ward off attackers. Starfish can regrow their arms if predators eat them. Hermit crabs hide their soft bodies inside shells that once belonged to sea snails.

Getting to Know Reefs

If you live in the southeastern United States, coral reefs may be on your doorstep. The coral kingdom is yours to explore with just a snorkel and diving mask. Always take an adult with you when you swim. Elsewhere in North America, visit your local aquarium to see reef animals. You can also look at Web sites on coral reefs.

Snorkeling is exciting. Always remember not to touch the fragile coral reef.

Sandy and rocky seashores and river **estuaries** are home to animals closely related to coral reef species. Your next trip to the seashore can become a wildlife expedition! Look for sea anemones, small fish, crabs, and starfish in tidal pools. Shrimp, crabs, and worms hide in the sand or under stones on the beach. Place your finds in a bucket of seawater while you study them. A magnifying glass will make it easier to see them. Afterward, put the animals back where you found them.

TOP TIPS FOR BEACH DETECTIVES

1 Rocks on the seashore can be very slippery. Be careful as you move around. Leave both hands free to grip the rocks by storing your possessions in a backpack.

2 When exploring tidal pools, place a diver's face mask on the water's surface. That will allow you to see below more clearly.

3 Do not touch sea urchins or stranded jellyfish. These animals can give you a painful sting.

Many aquariums let you get up close to some sea creatures.

Glossary

algae Plantlike living things. Many algae are tiny; others, such as seaweeds, are much larger.

camouflage Colors and patterns that help an animal blend in with its surroundings.

carrion Dead meat.

estuary The mouth of a river where the freshwater current and ocean's tide meet.

filter feeder An animal that sifts water for algae or animals to eat.

lagoon An area of calm water between a reef crest and shore.

parasites Living things that take food or shelter from their host and usually harm it in return.

pollute To put harmful substances in the air, water, or soil.

polyps Small water animals with tube-shaped bodies and tentacles.

predators Animals that hunt other animals for food.

prey An animal that is eaten by another animal.

species A group of plants or animals that are similar and can produce young together.

Index

algae 15, 24, 28

angelfish 7, 20, 26

barracuda 6, 7, 25, 26, 27

brain coral 7, 10, 11

butterfly fish 7, 18

Christmas tree worm 12

clam 12, 14

cleaner wrasse 22

clown fish 23

copepod 7, 26

coral polyp 6, 8, 10, 14, 15

cuttlefish 21

elkhorn coral 9

flounder 21, 27

hermit crab 6, 29

octopus 6, 21

parrot fish 7, 15, 20

remora 6, 23

sea anemone 6, 12, 14, 23

sea fan 7, 11

sea horse 16

sea slug 6, 13, 15, 29

sergeant major fish 19

shark 6, 7, 23, 26, 27

shrimp 6, 24, 26, 31

soft coral 11

sponge 5, 6, 7, 12

starfish 6, 13, 15, 29, 31

stony coral 11

surgeonfish 7, 29

tiger grouper 27

whale shark 24

zooplankton 13, 14